AF689790

Eye Movement Desensitization and Reprocessing (EMDR)

A Step-by-Step Patient Guide to the 8 Phases, Readiness Checklists, and Session Tracking (Worksheets Included)

mf

copyright © 2026 Patrick Marshwell

All rights reserved No part of this book may be reproduced, or stored in a retrieval system, or transmitted in any form or by any means, electronic, mechanical, photocopying, recording, or otherwise, without express written permission of the publisher.

Disclaimer

By reading this guide, you are accepting the terms of this disclaimer in full. If you do not agree with these terms, please do not read or use this guide.

All content within this guide is provided for informational and educational purposes only and should not be considered medical, psychological, or other professional advice. The author is not a doctor, physician, psychologist, psychotherapist, counselor, or licensed healthcare provider. Reading or using this guide does not establish any form of a patient-client or therapeutic relationship.

Always consult with a physician, licensed therapist, or other qualified health professional regarding any questions or concerns you may have about your physical or mental health. Never disregard professional advice or delay seeking it because of something you have read in this guide.

The information presented in this guide is based on general research, personal interpretation, and publicly available sources. While reasonable efforts have been made to provide accurate and current information, the author and publisher make no representations or warranties about the completeness, accuracy, reliability, or suitability of the content. The author and publisher shall not be held liable for any errors, omissions, or outcomes related to the use of this guide.

You acknowledge that you are solely responsible for how you choose to use the information in this guide and that any actions you take based on this content are undertaken at your own risk. The publisher shall not be liable for any loss, injury, or damages arising from the application of any information provided herein.

This guide does not promise or guarantee any specific result, outcome, or improvement in well-being, mental health, or nervous system regulation. Individual results may vary.

Where applicable, any tools, concepts, or names mentioned are the property of their respective owners and are used strictly for identification or illustrative purposes. Their mention does not imply endorsement. Any individuals shown in the cover or promotional images are stock photography models, and image rights have been obtained through appropriate licensing agreements.

Table of Contents

Introduction

Trauma can disrupt daily life, and finding effective help can feel confusing due to the overwhelming range of therapies, advice, and opinions available. Many people start their recovery journey uncertain where to begin or hesitant about what comes next. Questions about personal readiness, what therapy sessions involve, and how one might react emotionally are common.

This uncertainty sometimes results in doubt or withdrawal before healing can happen. Without a clear idea of therapy expectations and timelines, distress can be prolonged rather than relieved. A step-by-step guide centered on the patient is essential to clarify the process and encourage engagement.

This guide explains what to expect from every stage of Eye Movement Desensitization and Reprocessing (EMDR) therapy by outlining its eight structured phases. The aim is to provide straightforward, practical support for patients, not clinical training for therapists.

While other resources may focus on professional theory or detailed protocol, this guide is specifically tailored to your needs as a patient: preparing for sessions, assessing your readiness, and actively participating in your treatment. Complex therapeutic decisions, trauma assessments, and case management remain the responsibility of your EMDR therapist; this guide helps you focus on your own role—self-preparation, self-assessment, meaningful participation, and monitoring your progress.

In this guide, you will learn:

- How EMDR therapy's eight phases build upon each other.
- How to use readiness checklists to assess your preparedness before starting each phase.
- How worksheets can help you track your thoughts, emotions, and significant experiences during each session.
- How to use practical tools such as charts and logs to organize notes, record emotional responses, and structure action plans for each phase.
- How to organize memories, beliefs, and distress ratings phase by phase, and when to share crucial information with your therapist.
- How to monitor shifts in emotions and bodily sensations, evaluate the reinforcement of positive beliefs, and use this information to assess your continued progress and healing opportunities.

This guide is not a replacement for therapy or clinical assessment. It is designed to complement your work with a qualified EMDR therapist by offering patient-friendly tools and instructions. Understanding what will happen, how to check your readiness, and how to document your journey puts you in a stronger, more active position to support your recovery.

Overview of EMDR Fundamentals

It is essential to understand its origins, scientific foundations, and what makes it unique among trauma therapies. This chapter provides a cohesive introduction to the history, fundamental concepts, and mechanisms at the heart of EMDR, giving you a solid foothold for the practical steps that follow in later chapters.

Timeline of EMDR Development and Evidence of Effectiveness

Eye Movement Desensitization and Reprocessing (EMDR) was first developed in the late 1980s by psychologist Francine Shapiro. This new method began when she noticed that certain eye movements seemed to reduce the distress associated with negative thoughts. Shapiro went on to systematically study this effect, creating a structured therapy protocol that was published in 198. EMDR evolved into a comprehensive, eight-phase approach that addresses trauma and other distressing life experiences by using standardized procedures and detailed phase structures.

Since its introduction, EMDR has accumulated an impressive evidence base. Numerous controlled studies have examined its effectiveness for treating trauma and post-traumatic stress disorder (PTSD). Multiple mental health organizations and professional associations now recognize EMDR as an evidence-based treatment for PTSD, alongside other gold-standard therapies.

Systematic reviews have found that EMDR often produces results at least as favorable as traditional cognitive-behavioral therapy (CBT), particularly for symptoms of acute and chronic trauma. It is one of the few therapies specifically recommended by international guidelines for the treatment of trauma-related conditions.

Along with its use in PTSD, ongoing research also supports EMDR's effectiveness for complicated grief, anxiety disorders, depression, and distress related to disturbing life events. While the most robust data are for trauma and PTSD, EMDR's application continues to grow as more is understood about its unique mechanisms and broad benefits.

Understanding Traumatic Memory and Maladaptive Memory Processing

Central to EMDR is the idea that many symptoms of trauma, anxiety, or distress stem from the way the brain stores and processes memories. When a person experiences a traumatic or overwhelming event, the details including images, sounds, emotions, and physical sensations can become “stuck” or “frozen” in memory pathways, rather than being integrated with other experiences or time. This maladaptive memory storage is different from ordinary memory processing, where experiences can be recalled without causing undue emotional or physical discomfort.

These unprocessed traumatic memories may be easily triggered even years later resulting in physical tension, intense emotions, negative self-beliefs, and disturbing mental images. Common symptoms include flashbacks, nightmares, emotional numbness, irritability, avoidance of reminders, and feelings of guilt or shame. In EMDR, these symptoms are seen as signs that the memory is stored in a raw, unprocessed form and hasn’t been neutralized or reconciled with more adaptive information.

EMDR works by targeting these maladaptively stored memories. The therapy guides you to recall “target memories” in a safe setting while using specific techniques to encourage the brain to reprocess the experience. Over time and with repeated sessions, previously disturbing memories become less emotionally charged and less likely to intrude upon daily life. This process helps link traumatic information with more adaptive beliefs and feelings, promoting healing and reducing symptoms.

Eye Movements, Tactile, and Auditory Methods

EMDR sets itself apart from other trauma-focused therapies by incorporating bilateral stimulation. This technique engages both hemispheres of the brain in a rhythmic, alternating manner typically achieved through controlled eye movements. In a session, the therapist will prompt you to bring distressing memories or thoughts to mind while guiding your eyes side to side, often by having you track their hand or a moving light.

While eye movements are the original and most widely used form, bilateral stimulation can also be achieved through other senses:

- ***Tactile***: Alternating taps or vibrations delivered to the hands (for example, holding buzzers that gently pulse left-right).
- ***Auditory***: Alternating sounds, like beeps or tones, played in one ear and then the other using headphones.

Patients and therapists may select the most suitable form of bilateral stimulation based on comfort, physical needs, or specific therapeutic goals. Research indicates that these alternating movements or sensations may help "unblock" stuck memories and assist the brain in processing fragmented or distressing material. The precise mechanisms are still under investigation, but leading theories suggest bilateral stimulation may reduce emotional intensity, increase cognitive flexibility, and encourage integration of stored information.

The flexibility to use eye movements, tapping, or audio signals means EMDR can be adapted for people with various physical or sensory needs, further increasing its accessibility.

EMDR Process Flowchart: The Eight Phases Step-By-Step

The EMDR protocol is built around eight distinct but interconnected phases. Each phase is designed to ensure safety, support gradual processing, and maximize the benefits of therapy. Understanding the entire sequence helps you anticipate what happens at each stage, reducing anxiety about the unknown and improving your ability to track progress.

Here is the step-by-step EMDR process:

1. ***History Taking (Phase 1)***: Gathering background information about your experiences, trauma history, and current symptoms. The therapist works with you to develop a treatment plan and identify target memories.
2. ***Preparation (Phase 2)***: Building therapeutic trust, explaining EMDR procedures, and developing emotional self-regulation skills. This phase emphasizes safety and coping techniques.
3. ***Assessment (Phase 3)***: Pinpointing a specific target memory, identifying negative and positive beliefs

associated with it, and rating your distress and belief strength.

4. ***Desensitization (Phase 4)***: Focusing on the target memory while engaging in bilateral stimulation. This phase reduces the memory's emotional charge and disruptive power.
5. ***Installation (Phase 5)***: Reinforcing a positive belief, strengthening its connection to the previously disturbing memory using bilateral stimulation.
6. ***Body Scan (Phase 6)***: Scanning the body for lingering physical tension or discomfort linked to the memory and reprocessing as needed.
7. ***Closure (Phase 7)***: Returning to a stable, calm state at the end of each session, using relaxation or grounding exercises and reviewing progress.
8. ***Reevaluation (Phase 8)***: Reviewing changes achieved, confirming memory distress has lessened and identifying new targets if necessary before the next session.

Quick-Reference Chart: EMDR's Unique Mechanisms vs. Other Trauma Therapies

To clarify what sets EMDR apart, here is a simple chart comparing its key mechanisms with those of other widely used trauma therapies. This can help you understand EMDR's distinctive features and why your therapist may recommend it over or alongside other approaches.

Table 1: EMDR Quick-Reference Chart

Therapy	Main Goal	Memory Proce-ssing Focus	Bilateral Stimula-tion	Cogni-tive Work	Direct Expo-sure
EMDR	Memory reproce-ssing, symptom relief	Yes	Yes (eye/ tactile/ audio)	Some, focused integra-tion	Indirect (memory recall)
Cognitive-Behavio-ral	Modify thoughts/ behaviors to reduce distress	Some-times, via discu-ssion	No	Extensive	Direct, through talking or imaginal exposure
Prolonged Exposure	Reduce fear through repeated exposure	No	No	Limited	Direct (detailed retelling)
Trauma-Focused CBT	Change thought patterns; build coping skills	Some-times	No	Extensive	Some, via narra-tives or assign-ments
Psychody namic/ Psycho-analytic	Insight and meaning-making	Some-times, through analysis	No	Moderate to extensive	Indirect or variable

Key Points of Difference:

- EMDR uniquely uses bilateral stimulation to enhance memory reprocessing.
- The approach does not require you to describe all details of traumatic memories out loud, which can make it more comfortable for some patients than therapies based on detailed exposure.

- While cognitive reframing is present in EMDR, the primary goal is to help the brain naturally reprocess stored memories, not just talk through them.
- EMDR phases provide a structured, phase-by-phase progression, offering both flexibility and a strong procedural framework.

EMDR stands out as a structured, evidence-based therapy specifically tailored for addressing trauma and distress at their roots. By directly targeting how traumatic memories are stored and by using the unique method of bilateral stimulation EMDR helps unlock stuck memories, reduce unnecessary emotional pain, and reinforce healthier self-beliefs and coping abilities. The research supporting EMDR's effectiveness is robust, particularly for trauma and PTSD, and its distinct structure allows for adaptability and patient participation throughout the entire healing process.

Understanding these fundamentals provides the clarity and confidence needed to approach EMDR step by step. In the chapters ahead, you will find practical checklists, worksheets, and process maps to guide you through each phase of therapy, always with your safety, autonomy, and progress as the central focus.

Phase 1—History Taking and Treatment Planning

The first phase of Eye Movement Desensitization and Reprocessing therapy (EMDR) sets the stage for all that follows. A thorough, well-organized history taking and careful treatment planning form the foundation for safe and effective trauma processing.

This chapter presents the practical tools and clarifying steps that patients can use to prepare for EMDR therapy, including worksheets, checklists, criteria tables, and sample planning forms. By actively participating in this preparatory process, you ensure your treatment is tailored to your unique needs, experiences, and personal goals.

Patient Preparation Worksheet for Gathering Trauma History and Identifying Target Memories

Active involvement in your EMDR history-taking process empowers you to clarify your background, spot potential therapy targets, and participate in collaborative planning with your therapist. A preparation worksheet can help you organize memories or themes, consider patterns of distress, and identify issues that require attention.

A typical worksheet is divided into useful sections:

- ***Significant Life Events***: Note major positive and negative events from childhood through adulthood, such as losses, accidents, bullying, relationship disruptions, and any singular traumatic incidents (like assault, natural disaster, or medical trauma).
- ***Recurring Distress***: List experiences, memories, or situations that repeatedly upset you or cause strong emotional or bodily reactions, even if you believe they "shouldn't" affect you anymore.
- ***Problematic Current Symptoms***: Record present-day problems that disrupt your wellbeing, such as panic attacks, nightmares, withdrawal, irritability, or specific triggers that interfere with your daily life.
- ***Potential Target Memories***: For EMDR, you do not need to name every trauma. Instead, try to remember brief "snapshots" of an image, sound, sensation, or phrase linked to the worst part of a memory. Jot down 2-5 of these "hot spots" that feel especially charged, confusing, or distressing.

The goal is not to recount or analyze every event in detail, but to start building a "target list" that can be refined with your therapist. Many individuals find just writing the outline of these memories or symptoms helps reduce unspoken anxiety about the process and increases feelings of agency within therapy.

Checklist for Selecting Appropriate Memories or Experiences for EMDR Processing

Not all experiences or memories are suitable for immediate EMDR processing. To choose appropriate targets, a checklist can help ensure safety, clarity, and suitability. **Consider the following when reviewing your memory list with your therapist:**

- Is the memory connected to current symptoms or distress?
- Can you recall a specific image or moment that feels unfinished, intrusive, or especially disturbing?
- Does thinking of this memory trigger strong emotions, bodily sensations, or negative beliefs about yourself?
- Are there memories that remain distressing despite time, talking, or previous efforts at resolution?
- Can you stay "present" when recalling this memory, or does it cause overwhelming dissociation or loss of contact with the present?
- Has your therapist checked that basic emotional regulation skills are in place for focusing on this memory safely?

Your therapist may help you "calibrate" which experiences feel ripe for processing and which need to wait until further preparation. This ensures that EMDR sessions focus on memories that most directly affect your current well-being and are manageable with your present coping skills.

Table of Exclusion Criteria and Situations Requiring Alternate Intervention Before EMDR

While EMDR is broadly effective, certain conditions or situations must be addressed before proceeding to full trauma processing. The following table summarizes common exclusion criteria and identifies when alternate or preliminary intervention is necessary:

Table 2: Exclusion Criteria Table

Criterion	Implication for EMDR	Alternate Action Needed
Active substance dependence or intoxication	Processing is unsafe/inhibited	Stabilization, addiction treatment
Current self-harm or suicidality	High risk; session destabilization likely	Crisis intervention, stabilization work
Severe dissociation (inability to remain oriented or present in session)	Ineffective, risk of retraumatization	Build grounding/coping skills, stabilization
Uncontrolled medical or neurological	Risk of physical harm or distress	Medical evaluation and stabilization

condition		
Acute psychosis or severe mania	Processing unlikely to be productive, may worsen symptoms	Psychiatric treatment, stabilization
Ongoing severe threat or unsafe living situation	Safety compromised, limited gains	Address immediate physical/situational safety

Your therapist will review these criteria during the intake and planning phase. If you fall under any exclusion category, EMDR trauma processing will be postponed, but supportive or preparatory work may still proceed until it is safe to begin the core phases.

Overview of Information Commonly Requested in Initial Therapist Intake

During your first meetings, EMDR therapists gather both broad and targeted information to design a safe and effective treatment plan. **You can expect questions and discussion that touch on:**

- ***Mental health history***: past diagnoses, treatments, hospitalizations, and outcomes.
- ***Medical history***: neurological or chronic health issues, head injuries, medications, sleep, and relevant physical health conditions.
- ***Family background***: family mental health histories, support systems, major losses, or conflict patterns.

- ***Trauma and stressor history***: significant distressing events, dates/ages, relationship to current symptoms, patterns of triggers.
- ***Strengths and coping resources***: what has previously helped you manage distress, including activities, relationships, spiritual or cultural anchors.
- ***Daily life impact***: work, school, and social functioning; how trauma currently affects your goals, relationships, and daily routines.
- ***Symptom checklist***: current experience of anxiety, depression, flashbacks, nightmares, substance use, and other relevant symptoms.
- ***Readiness for therapy***: motivation, concerns, personal goals for therapy, potential obstacles, and hopes for change.

Some intake forms may also ask for current safety concerns (regarding self-harm, suicidality, or domestic violence), preferred communication style, previous response to therapy, and any desired accommodations (such as for sensory issues or language).

Being prepared to share this information even if you choose to pace or withhold certain details helps your therapist create an attuned, individualized treatment plan, and ensures the therapy unfolds at the pace that works best for you.

Sample Treatment Planning Form to Clarify Goals, Concerns, and Session Expectations

A collaborative treatment planning form can make Phase 1 more concrete, translating history and target selection into a focused roadmap for your EMDR work. Sample sections of such a form include:

1. ***Treatment Goals***: List what you most hope to achieve. Examples include "reduce frequency of panic attacks," "less distress when remembering [specific event]," or "improve self-esteem and comfort in relationships."
2. ***Symptom Priorities***: Rank or describe the symptoms or problems you'd like help with first, or those that feel most urgent or disruptive (e.g., nightmares, avoidance behaviors, sudden emotional outbursts).
3. ***Target Memories and Experiences***: List initial "target" memories, events, or persistent beliefs (e.g., "I am unsafe," "I am powerless," or "I am to blame") that are high on your priority list for EMDR processing.
4. ***Strengths and Supports***: Describe personal resources, trusted individuals, or coping tools you can rely on during treatment (connecting with friends, practicing mindfulness, using creative expression, etc.).
5. ***Session Preferences and Concerns***: Note how you'd like sessions to unfold (preferred pace, comfort with self-disclosure, sensitivity to physical/tactile stimuli, technological aids, etc.). Record concerns or fears

about EMDR such as being overwhelmed, worried about "losing control," or not remembering important details.

6. ***Frequency and Scheduling***: Record practical session preferences how often you wish to meet, ideal session times, and any needed accommodations for accessibility or privacy.

By filling out such a form and reviewing it together with your therapist, you sharpen your sense of control and intentionality in the process. These written goals and preferences serve as a compass, keeping your EMDR work focused and contained when strong emotions or uncertainties inevitably arise.

EMDR's initial phase is not something that happens "to" you; it is most effective when done "with" you. Your willingness to reflect, document, and share relevant details from your past and present directly shapes your therapy's direction and your sense of safety. Using the worksheets, checklists, and forms described above supports transparency making sure both you and your therapist are clear about what is most important, what is safe to address, and where to focus your efforts.

Documenting and organizing these elements will help you track your progress, revisit initial goals as you move through EMDR's later phases, and identify new targets as you grow. Most importantly, it ensures that you begin processing with as much information, collaboration, and confidence as possible.

Once history taking and treatment plans are in place, the next phase of EMDR focuses on enhancing your sense of safety and readying you for active memory processing. The foundational work you put in during Phase 1 makes the step-by-step process that follows less overwhelming and more effective. With these Phase 1 tools at your side, you are well-positioned to work with your therapist to develop the skills needed for stability, resilience, and meaningful healing.

Phase 2—Preparation and Building Skills for Safety

Phase 2 of Eye Movement Desensitization and Reprocessing (EMDR) therapy is centered on ensuring you are emotionally ready and have the coping skills required for safe and productive memory processing. This chapter takes you through systematic steps and practical tools to assess your preparedness, practice stabilization techniques, and establish a secure therapeutic foundation. Here, you will find checklists, worksheets, and charts designed for active use before you begin the core trauma processing phases of EMDR.

Self-Assessment Checklist for Identifying Emotional Readiness and Personal Coping Skills

A hallmark of effective EMDR therapy is your active participation in preparation. Before processing distressing memories, it's essential to gauge your current ability to handle strong feelings, manage anxiety, and communicate your needs. Use the following checklist to self-assess emotional readiness and identify coping strengths or gaps. **<u>Share these responses with your therapist to tailor your preparation:</u>**

- Do I have experience using at least one healthy coping skill (breathing, grounding, or relaxation) when distressed?
- Can I generally recognize escalating emotions and label what I am feeling?
- Am I able to return to a calmer state after emotional upset, even if it takes some effort or support?
- When anxious or overwhelmed, do I have techniques (self-talk, movement, creative outlets, support calls) that help me feel safer?
- Can I let my therapist know when distress is rising, or do I find it difficult to ask for breaks or changes in session?
- Do overwhelming thoughts or emotions make me "check out" (dissociate) or feel detached from reality?
- What have I learned about ways I effectively calm or support myself in the past—inside or outside of therapy?

If most answers are "yes," you are likely ready to move forward with the additional skills training provided in Phase 2. If there are "no" responses or areas of uncertainty, discuss these with your therapist so they can adjust preparation accordingly. Building this honest self-awareness is a key protective factor against becoming overwhelmed during processing in later EMDR phases.

List of Common Relaxation Techniques and Stabilization Exercises Practiced in Phase 2

Building a personal toolkit of relaxation and stabilization strategies is a major focus of this phase. You may be guided through several techniques in session and asked to practice them at home. These exercises help reduce anxiety, increase a sense of control, and form a "landing pad" for returning to baseline after recalling difficult material. Common methods include:

- ***Controlled Breathing***: Practicing slow, deep belly breathing to lower heart rate and decrease tension.
- ***Mindful Grounding***: Focusing on sensory input (touch, sound, sight) to bring attention back to the present moment—naming 5 things you see, 4 you feel, and so on.
- ***Progressive Muscle Relaxation***: Systematically tensing and releasing muscle groups to notice and reduce physical tension.
- ***Safe Place Visualization***: Imagining a calm, comforting location in your mind, using sensory detail to evoke feelings of safety and peace.

- ***Body Scan***: Paying focused awareness to different parts of your body, noticing sensations, and consciously relaxing tense areas.
- ***"Container" Imagery***: Visualizing a secure box or vault to mentally set aside distressing thoughts or memories temporarily.
- ***Anchoring Movements***: Pairing physical gestures (such as pressing thumb to finger or swaying gently) with relaxation to reinforce safety cues.

During Phase 2, it's normal to experiment with several techniques and notice which feel natural, effective, or require more practice. Over time, these skills become foundational supports used throughout all later EMDR phases, especially after intense emotional work.

Worksheet for Identifying Personal Resources and Establishing an Imagery Safe Place

Recognizing what helps you feel strong, grounded, or supported is crucial. Use a worksheet like the following to clarify your unique resources and lay the groundwork for customized coping in session.

Part 1: Personal Resources Inventory

- People I trust to support me emotionally (list names or relationships).

- Activities that soothe me or make me feel competent (music, pets, reading, exercise).
- Reminders or objects that bring comfort or security (photos, scents, meaningful objects).
- Affirmations or beliefs that help when I am struggling ("This feeling will pass," "I am not alone").
- Techniques I use (or could try) to ground myself when anxious.

Part 2: Creating a Safe Place Visualization

1. Imagine a real or imagined place that feels perfectly safe, relaxing, or pleasant. Close your eyes and picture as many details as possible:
    - What do you see, hear, smell, and feel in this place?
    - What colors, sounds, scents, or textures are most vivid?
    - Is anyone else present, or are you alone in this image?
    - How does your body feel when you "step into" this place?

2. Practice returning to this place in your mind when you notice rising tension or after emotional work in session. The "safe place" is not just a mental escape, but a deliberately created internal resource you can strengthen with repeated practice.

You may customize your safe place with your therapist, practice entering and enhancing it between sessions, and refine it over time. Having such a resource often makes patients feel less anxious about confronting difficult memories since they have a reliable way to regain calm.

Chart of Safety Agreements and What to Do if Distress Escalates

To minimize the risk of becoming emotionally overwhelmed, Phase 2 includes creating a clear agreement on safety procedures and what you and your therapist will do if distress grows too high, whether in session or between appointments.

Table 3: Sample Safety Agreement Chart:

If I Notice...	My Response	My Therapist's Response
Rising anxiety or overwhelm	Signal with word/gesture	Pause, check in, offer break
Physical symptoms (shaking, numbness)	Name sensation aloud	Guide grounding exercise
Racing/fragmented thoughts	Request containment	Assist with imagery/containment technique
Urge to "leave" or dissociate	Verbalize what's happening	Encourage use of safe place/pause
Unable to regain calm after attempts	Request session pause/end	Support closure, review next steps

Safety agreements reassure you that you're not expected to "push through" extreme discomfort. Instead, you have clear, prearranged steps and signals to guide recovery and maintain emotional equilibrium. Reviewing this chart together perhaps at the start of each session deepens your sense of control.

Explanation of the Therapeutic Alliance and Expectations for Patient-Therapist Communication

A strong, transparent therapeutic relationship is the cornerstone of successful EMDR, especially during the preparation phase. Your therapist's role is to be a collaborative partner, offering empathy and nonjudgment while guiding you through exercises, skill-building, and emotional groundwork. At the same time, it is important for you to communicate openly about feelings, preferences, fears, and difficulties encountered in or between sessions.

Here's what you can expect in the therapeutic alliance during Phase 2:

- ***Mutual Respect***: Your therapist will value your experiences, choices, and boundaries, adjusting the pace and method of therapy based on your feedback and needs.
- ***Teamwork Approach***: The process is collaborative. You'll be encouraged to voice doubts, ask questions, and direct the focus toward what feels manageable on any given day.
- ***Clear Communication Channels***: You and your therapist will practice giving and receiving feedback

about comfort levels, effectiveness of stabilization exercises, and readiness to proceed to later phases.

- ***Transparency About Process***: Your provider will explain why certain techniques are being used, what each step is intended to accomplish, and how your input shapes the treatment path.
- ***Commitment to Safety***: At any sign of distress, the therapist will return attention to stabilization and calming techniques, ensuring you do not feel forced to revisit distressing memories until adequate resources are in place.

The alliance is not simply "being nice"—it is a professional relationship characterized by trust, mutual goal-setting, and a shared commitment to your autonomy and safety throughout EMDR.

Bringing It All Together: Your Phase 2 Checklist

As you progress through Phase 2, rely on the following stepwise checklist to ensure comprehensive preparation:

1. Complete the emotional readiness self-assessment and discuss results with your therapist.
2. Learn and practice at least two relaxation or grounding exercises; identify one as your "go-to" technique.
3. Fill out the personal resources worksheet, including developing your safe place imagery.

4. Review and sign off on a safety agreement chart—knowing exactly how distress will be handled in session.
5. Establish a regular pattern of open communication with your therapist; practice expressing needs, concerns, and feedback after each stabilization exercise.

If any area feels uncertain or incomplete, revisit that step with your therapist. Thorough preparation here increases your resilience, strengthens your coping toolkit, and creates the safety necessary for effective trauma processing in future EMDR phases. Through these strategies, Phase 2 transforms anxiety about "going deeper" into a sense of mastery and collaborative support, laying the groundwork for genuine healing and progress.

Phase 3—Assessment and Target Memory Identification

Phase 3 of Eye Movement Desensitization and Reprocessing (EMDR) therapy serves as the transition into the core trauma-processing work. The focus now shifts from general preparation and safety to the selection and in-depth organization of the distressing memories you wish to process.

In this phase, you will use structured methods to examine how specific experiences have impacted your thoughts, beliefs, emotions, and body. By capturing these details, you and your therapist lay a clear path for effective subsequent EMDR phases and gain practical tools to track your reactions and progress.

Framework for Organizing Disturbing Memories, Negative Beliefs, and Desired Beliefs

Phase 3 is the systematic assessment and organization of the target memories (often called "target scenes" or "targets") you want to address in therapy. This framework goes beyond simply remembering what happened; it involves pinpointing the associated negative core beliefs and consciously specifying the beliefs or feelings you would rather hold about yourself. This approach allows for a nuanced understanding of how past events are rooted in your current thoughts and helps reveal the beliefs you hope to install in place of the old, limiting ones.

The assessment process may begin by listing memories that still cause emotional or physical distress, such as flashbacks, intrusive images, or intense emotional reactions in daily life. With your therapist, select one memory at a time to focus on. **For each selected memory, identify:**

- A clear description of the target incident or moment (often a "worst moment" or a scene that encapsulates the distress)
- The negative cognition (NC): a self-directed belief the memory triggers (e.g., "I am powerless," "I am unsafe," "I'm not good enough")
- The positive cognition (PC): a self-affirming belief you would like to replace the old one (e.g., "I am in control now," "I am safe," "I am worthy")
- The specific emotions the memory brings up (fear, shame, anger, sadness)
- The locations in your body where you feel that distress (such as tightness in the chest, tension in the jaw, or queasiness)

Documenting this information for each target memory creates an organized map for later processing and enables you to track direct changes as therapy progresses.

SUD (Subjective Units of Distress) Rating Scale Tracking Sheet

To measure the intensity of your current distress linked to each target memory, EMDR therapy relies on the Subjective Units of Distress (SUD) rating scale. The SUD scale is a self-reported measure ranging from 0 to 10 where 0 means "no disturbance or distress at all," and 10 indicates "the worst possible distress you could imagine." This tool is simple yet powerful; it helps both you and your therapist quantify how much a memory currently affects you and monitor your emotional changes as processing unfolds.

Below is a practical template for tracking SUD scores for each memory:

Table 4: SUD Rating Scale Tracking Sheet Template

Target Memory Description	**Date**	**SUD Score (0-10)**	**Notes on Emotions or Response**
Example: Car accident at age 17	04/12/2024	8	Tight chest, fear, shame
______	—	–	______
______	—	–	______

You are encouraged to fill in your SUD level at the start of each session, after describing the memory, and after each round of EMDR bilateral stimulation (in later phases) to watch your distress decrease over time.

VOC (Validity of Cognition) Scale Completion Example for Positive Belief Assessment

While the SUD scale tracks distress, the Validity of Cognition (VOC) scale is used to rate how true a positive cognition feels to you right now, in connection to the target memory. The VOC scale typically ranges from 1 ("completely false") to 7 ("completely true"). This measure contrasts your initial negative belief with the new, more adaptive belief you aim to truly feel.

Here's an example of how you might complete the VOC assessment:

- Positive belief: "I am safe now."
- While holding the memory in mind, ask yourself: "How true does this statement feel about myself right now on a scale of 1 to 7?"
    - 1 = Completely False
    - 7 = Completely True

You might note:

Table 5: VOC Scale Completion Example

Target Memory	Positive Cognition	VOC Score (1-7)	Notes
Car accident at 17	I am safe now	2	Still feel vulnerable
______	__	_	______
______	__	_	______

Over time, you should see your VOC score increase as EMDR therapy progresses, reflecting a genuine shift in how you relate to yourself in the context of old memories.

Fields to record detailed descriptions of target scenes and associated physical sensations

EMDR's impact depends on the richness and accuracy with which you capture the full scope of your experience. That's why it's vital to provide detailed descriptions of not just the factual content of the memory, but the "snapshot" or specific image that sums up the distress of the so-called "target scene." Alongside the visual and narrative content, pay close attention to sensations in your body as you recall the memory. Trauma is often stored not just as thoughts but as physical feeling, such as muscle tension, racing heartbeat, nausea, or numbness.

A structured worksheet for this purpose might include:

- ***Target Scene Description***: (Write in as much sensory detail as possible. Example: "I see the headlights in the dark, hear screeching brakes, notice the smell of burnt rubber, and feel my arms gripping the steering wheel.")
- ***Emotions Felt***: (List primary emotions: terror, guilt, panic, etc.)
- ***Physical Sensations***: (Describe precisely: "Numbness in hands, tightness in chest, pounding heart.")

Recording this information allows you to observe patterns (such as recurring feelings of tightness or persistent sadness) and helps your therapist tailor interventions to your specific needs as you move through each session.

Template for listing negative and positive self-statements connected to each target memory

A core feature of Phase 3 is documenting the interplay between negative and positive self-statements (cognitions) linked to your target memories. Negative cognitions are not just passing thoughts; they are deep-seated beliefs arising from trauma that often continue to influence your self-image and expectations. Positive cognitions are statements you consciously select as healthier replacements ones that better reflect your strengths, values, and current reality.

You can use a simple template to organize these for each identified target:

Table 6: Negative and Positive Self-Statements Template

Target Memory	Negative Cognition	Positive Cognition
Car accident at 17	"I am powerless."	"I am in control now."
________	________	________
________	________	________

Your therapist will help you clarify both types of statements, ensuring they are specific and meaningful to you. During later phases, these self-statements provide the focus for the installation of positive cognitions and further desensitization work.

Bringing the Assessment Tools Together: Step-by-Step Instructions

To make the most of Phase 3, follow this systematic approach—completing each part in dialogue with your therapist:

1. ***List Candidate Memories***: Jot down experiences that continue to trigger distress or interfere with daily life. Focus on single "episodes" or moments rather than entire life periods.
2. ***Describe Each Target Scene in Detail***: For each memory, write out sensory details and the "worst part"

to clarify exactly what image or moment you will target.

3. ***Identify Negative Cognition***: Note the negative self-belief that comes up automatically with this memory.
4. ***Identify Positive Cognition***: Select an adaptive, self-supporting belief you would prefer to feel true about yourself.
5. ***Assess Current SUD and VOC***: Rate each target's SUD (0–10) and initial VOC (1–7), recording scores on your worksheet.
6. ***List Emotions and Physical Sensations***: Describe what emotions and body sensations the memory activates.
7. ***Track Changes Over Time***: After each EMDR session (or every few weeks), revisit your SUD and VOC ratings for each memory to notice progress, setbacks, or areas for more focus.

If you find it difficult to identify negative or positive cognitions, or to pin down body sensations, do not worry many people need practice and guidance. Use the prompts and templates provided, and talk openly with your therapist about points of confusion.

Additional Tips for Effective Phase 3 Documentation

- Keep your worksheets in a private, accessible place so you can update them after sessions.

- If a memory feels too vague, focus on the strongest image or feeling that stands out rather than worrying about full accuracy.
- Practice “checking in” with your body by closing your eyes and noticing subtle sensations: Is your jaw clenched? Do you feel warmth, coolness, or numbness anywhere?
- If SUD or VOC scores don’t seem to change, log this honestly—it’s valuable information for adjusting your therapy plan.

Phase 3 of EMDR is foundational for effective trauma processing. Using a structured framework to organize memories, beliefs, and reactions empowers you to move through each session with clarity and purpose. The SUD and VOC scales, in combination with detailed descriptions and self-statement templates, function as both measurement tools and reflective exercises, helping you and your therapist assess progress and adjust the course of therapy as needed. Embrace this assessment phase as a partnership one that equips you for the deeper emotional healing phases ahead and sets a clear, actionable roadmap for your EMDR journey.

Phase 4—Desensitization and Bilateral Stimulation

Phase 4 of EMDR, known as Desensitization, is the heart of the therapy process. It's here that you will begin to notice significant shifts in how distressing memories affect you both emotionally and physically. During this phase, you will participate in focused exercises using bilateral stimulation often through eye movements while holding the target memory, emotion, or belief in mind. The goal is to help reduce the intensity of distress, decrease negative emotional charge, and support your brain in reprocessing traumatic or disturbing experiences so that they no longer dominate your present.

Step-by-step guide for participating in bilateral stimulation exercises

Bilateral stimulation is a structured process guided by the therapist, but your active participation is central. The following steps outline what you can expect and how to make the most of this phase as a patient:

1. ***Preparation***: You'll be asked to bring the target memory or image to mind, along with its associated negative belief, emotions, and physical sensations. This information—the output from your Phase 3 worksheets—serves as your starting point.
2. ***Baseline SUD Rating***: Before bilateral stimulation begins, you will rate your current distress using the Subjective Units of Distress (SUD) scale (0–10). This rating captures how disturbing the memory feels at the outset.
3. ***Selection of Bilateral Stimulation Method***: Your therapist will decide, often collaboratively, which form of bilateral stimulation to use. Most commonly, this involves tracking the therapist's fingers or a moving light with your eyes. However, tactile alternatives (such as alternating tapping on the hands or knees) and auditory signals (such as sounds moving from ear to ear with headphones) may also be used, depending on your comfort and what is available.
4. ***Focus and Stimulation Cycle***: While focusing on the "worst part" of the target memory and connected negative belief, you'll follow the therapist's cues for a cycle of bilateral stimulation. Typically, this lasts about 20–30 seconds per set, but the duration and frequency may vary based on your needs and responses.
5. ***Brief Reporting and Reflection***: After each stimulation set, the therapist will prompt you to briefly

describe any changes, images, thoughts, feelings, or physical sensations that arise. There's no right or wrong answer—your task is simply to notice and report.

6. ***SUD Reassessment***: At points throughout the process, especially after a few stimulation cycles, you will be asked to re-rate your SUD score. This helps both you and the therapist track how much your distress changes during the phase.
7. ***Continued Sets and Check-Ins***: Steps 4–6 are repeated, often with minor adjustments based on your feedback. The goal is to continue until your SUD score drops to a low or tolerable level, and until you notice a significant decrease in your distress response.
8. ***Closure (if needed)***: If your distress does not significantly reduce during this session, or if you become overly distressed, the therapist will guide you through self-soothing or containment exercises and ensure you return to a stable emotional state before concluding.

Each of these steps is collaboratively navigated. Your openness, willingness to notice your internal experience, and honest reporting are crucial. If you're uncertain about what to say during check-ins, simply describe the sensations, images, or "pieces" of memory that come to mind even if they seem unrelated or surprising.

Chart for tracking SUD scores before, during, and after stimulation cycles

To objectively monitor progress, it's helpful to keep a structured chart of your SUD ratings as you undergo bilateral stimulation cycles. Here is a recommended format for your worksheets:

Table 7: SUD Score Tracking Chart

Stimulation Set Number	Start of Set SUD	Notes on Change After Set
1	8	Felt image fade, stomach less tense
2	7	Thought shifted to being safe; less fear
3	5	Tension in jaw, now neutral
4	3	Memory seems distant

Use the SUD scale after each set or every few sets, as guided by your therapist. Documenting changes, however small, adds clarity to your experience and encourages a sense of progress over time.

Rules of thumb for identifying indications to pause or terminate stimulation

While bilateral stimulation is usually safe and empowering, there are clear signals that you and your therapist should pause, slow down, or in some cases stop altogether. **Familiarity with these signs helps you advocate for your comfort and safety:**

- ***SUD Score Spikes Up Rapidly***: If your distress level suddenly escalates rather than decreases, alert the therapist immediately. It's sometimes necessary to pause and recalibrate the approach.
- ***Overwhelming Emotions or Dissociation***: If you experience extreme fear, anger, numbness, or a sense of disconnect from reality or your body, tell your therapist. These are indications to stop stimulation and ground yourself.
- ***Physical Symptoms***: Strong symptoms such as dizziness, nausea, headaches, or shaking may require a pause or switch in technique.
- ***Mental Block or "Blankness"***: Sometimes patients feel mentally stuck or unable to access any thoughts, images, or sensations. This may mean the current memory is too charged or needs a different processing approach.
- ***Safety or Fatigue***: Feeling exhausted, unsafe, or unwell at any point is a sign to pause. The therapist can guide you through a stabilization or closure exercise when needed.

It is always appropriate to request a break, ask for a change in method, or stop the process if you are uncomfortable. Open collaboration ensures the tempo and structure of EMDR matches your individual needs and emotional stat.

List of possible emotional, physical, or cognitive responses during this phase

The desensitization phase often brings up a wide variety of sensations and reactions most of which are normal and expected. Being aware of these possibilities can help you recognize that your experience is part of the change process, not a sign of something going wrong. Possible responses include:

Emotional:

- Sudden waves of sadness, anger, relief, or fear as pieces of the memory are processed
- Brief emotional "flashes" you can't always name or explain
- Growing calmness or indifference toward the previously distressing memory

Physical:

- Tingling, warmth, or coolness in the arms, legs, chest, or face
- Muscle relaxation (jaw loosening, shoulders dropping) or short-term tension
- Changes in breathing or heart rate
- Sensations of heaviness or lightness
- Temporary aches, headaches, stomach "flutter," or nausea

Cognitive:

- New insights or connections ("I never realized it reminded me of…")
- Fragments of memory, images, or sounds that seem unrelated at first
- Shifting beliefs about yourself or the memory ("It's not my fault.")
- Vividness of images shrinking, becoming blurry or fading
- Thoughts feeling "lighter" or less tangled

Sometimes you may also notice a temporary intensification of symptoms before relief ("it gets worse before it gets better"). This is common and signals that your mind is working actively to reorganize and process the distressing material.

Sample worksheet for documenting changes in reactions after each stimulation set

To make the most of Phase 4, use a worksheet to systematically record your reactions and monitor shifts over time. This documentation is both a therapeutic tool and a reflective practice for your own sense of progress. Here's a sample:

Table 8: Sample Worksheet

Stimulation Set #	SUD Before	Description of Image/ Emotion/ Body Sensation	SUD After	Notable Change

1	8	Picture of accident, pressure in chest	7	Pressure lessened, image smaller
2	7	Tears, sadness, stomach queasy	6	Sadness lighter, focus less sharp
3	6	Thought: "I couldn't stop it," jaw tight	4	Jaw discomfort faded, sense of relief

You may complete this worksheet during pauses between sets or immediately after the session, depending on your therapist's routine. The goal is not perfect recall but honest reflection on what shifted even if it seems subtle or confusing.

Phase 4 of EMDR marks the transition from describing and planning to actively transforming your relationship with traumatic or distressing memories. By following a structured cycle of focusing on the target, engaging in bilateral stimulation, and systematically tracking your distress and subjective experience, you create space for genuine cognitive and emotional change.

Key strategies for success in this phase include attentively monitoring SUD scores before and after stimulation cycles, using worksheets to capture evolving reactions, and understanding both the typical responses and clear signals for pausing or adjusting the process. Remember, the variety of responses emotional, physical, or cognitive—is part of the natural range. Communicate openly with your therapist, and use the provided tracking tools to notice progress over time.

Through careful attention to each step and an honest approach to documenting changes, Phase 4 sets the stage for deep desensitization and lays the foundation for installing new, adaptive beliefs and feelings in subsequent phases.

Phase 5—Installation of Positive Cognition

The fifth phase of EMDR, called Installation, centers on shifting from reducing distress about a particular memory to building and strengthening a new, adaptive belief about oneself. After the emotional and physical intensity of Phase 4 has diminished, the Installation phase supports you in cultivating positive cognition statements about yourself that you want to truly believe and embody when recalling the previously distressing event.

In this chapter, you will learn how to clearly identify your positive cognition, track changes in the believability of that cognition, choose affirming statements that genuinely fit, and systematically link them to your target memories. Tools and worksheets are provided to help you notice shifts in emotion, physical sensation, or mental imagery as the new meaning becomes established.

Positive cognition identification checklist

A crucial first step in this phase is identifying a positive cognition that feels meaningful and plausible within the context of your target memory. This statement acts as a healthy, adaptive belief you wish to hold about yourself—such as "I am strong," "I can handle this," or "I am safe now." The positive cognition serves as a counterpoint to the negative belief that was linked to the traumatic memory in earlier phases. **To help select the best statement, use the following checklist:**

- Does this statement reflect how I would like to feel about myself or the situation now?
- Is the statement phrased in a positive, empowering way ("I can," "I am," "I deserve") rather than as a negation of the old belief?
- Does it feel at least somewhat believable? While it's normal if the statement doesn't feel fully true yet, you should have some openness to it.
- Is the statement broad enough to have meaning, but still specific to the experience or memory being targeted?
- Can I say the statement aloud or to myself without strong internal resistance or distress?
- When I reflect on the target memory, does this statement feel like it could apply even if only partially?

Completing this checklist ensures that your chosen positive cognition is relevant, supportive, and useful for reprocessing. If a statement feels flat or false, discuss possible alternatives with your therapist.

Progress form for tracking changes in VOC scores during installation

The Validity of Cognition (VOC) scale is a standard tool in EMDR for measuring how strongly you believe the positive cognition you've chosen. It uses a 7-point scale, with 1 being "completely false" and 7 meaning "completely true." During Phase 5, you will assess and re-assess your VOC score to monitor how installation is progressing.

A typical progress form for this phase might look like:

Table 9: VOC Scores

Installation Set #	VOC Score Before	Notes on Change	VOC Score After
1	3	Felt some hope; phrase still awkward	4
2	4	Image less sharp, belief "maybe true"	5
3	5	Statement feels warmer, less forced	6
4	6	Smiles, genuine agreement emerges	7

Tracking your VOC scores at different points helps you and your therapist see, in real-time, how the positive belief strengthens. You will usually be prompted to check your

VOC after each brief set of bilateral stimulation focused on the positive cognition.

Guidance for choosing supportive positive statements that feel genuine

One of the most impactful aspects of Phase 5 is learning how to choose and work with positive cognitions that actually feel attainable and supportive. It is normal if your initial attempt at stating something positive feels awkward or artificial. Often, the first statement is a "rough draft," and through discussion with your therapist or on your worksheet, you may notice aspects that don't fit or phrases that need refinement.

Here are helpful guidelines for refining your positive cognition:

- ***Check for Language***: Make sure your chosen phrase uses your own words. Avoid "therapy language" or statements that sound generic.
- ***Test for Emotional Resonance***: Say the statement in your mind while picturing the target memory. Notice whether you feel a connection, or if anything inside you objects strongly. Modify the statement if needed.
- ***Stay Realistic***: An affirmative statement doesn't need to be perfect or overly optimistic. For example, "I did the best I could" might fit better than "I was never hurt."

- ***Honor Ambivalence***: If a belief feels partially true but you have doubts, it can be helpful (and more powerful) to adapt the language—for example, "I'm learning that I am safe now" rather than "I am totally safe."
- ***Feedback Loop***: Allow yourself to adjust the statement through several iterations. Sometimes the best fit emerges only after exploring related words or images.

Remember, EMDR is not about forced positive thinking but about genuinely rewiring beliefs as your mind processes and integrates new information. Be honest with your therapist about how the statement lands, and be patient as it shifts.

Grid for correlating positive beliefs with targeted memories

To help you visualize and organize your progress, use a grid that maps which positive beliefs you are installing in relation to the specific memories or situations being processed. This approach builds clarity and allows you to see if certain beliefs help more in some contexts than others.

Table 10: Sample Grid Format

Target Memory or Event	Negative Cognition	Positive Cognition	VOC Change Observed
School bullying incident	"I am powerless"	"I can stand up for myself"	2 → 6
Car accident	"I am not safe"	"I am safe now"	3 → 7
Argument with parent	"I am unlovable"	"I am worthy of love"	4 → 6

Filling out this grid helps you track patterns, identify which beliefs are easiest to install, and note which memories benefit most from new positive meanings. It can also guide future sessions if further work is needed.

Worksheet to record shifts in emotion, somatic response, or mental imagery as installation occurs

EMDR Installation is holistic; it's not just about changing what you think, but about noticing how your entire experience changes as the new belief takes hold. To maximize insight and provide useful feedback for your therapist, use a worksheet during Phase 5 to record shifts in emotion, body sensations, or mental pictures that arise.

Table 11: Sample Tracking Shift Worksheet

Installation Set #	Positive Cognition Focused On	Pre-Set Emotion/ Body Sensation/ Image	Post-Set Change Observed
1	"I am safe now"	Low-grade fear, shoulder pain, memory of crash	Shoulders relaxed, calmer breath, image less vivid
2	"I am safe now"	Neutral feeling, slight tension	Lightness in chest, smile, positive mental image
3	"I am safe now"	Content, at ease	Warmth in body, memory loses negative charge

This documentation provides concrete evidence that emotional and physical shifts align with the strengthening of the new belief. It also highlights when further processing may be necessary, for example, if distressing body sensations persist or the positive cognition remains hard to believe.

Installation in Practice: What to Expect

During Phase 5, the therapist will guide you to focus on the target memory and your chosen positive statement. Bilateral stimulation, just as in previous phases, is used to "install" the new belief. Sets are briefer and less emotionally intense than in desensitization, and the focus is on observing how true the positive cognition feels. As your belief increases (reflected in rising VOC scores), many patients report physical relaxation, a sense of warmth, new insights, or a noticeable decrease in the emotional "sting" of the memory.

Use your progress forms, grid, and worksheets to track your VOC scores, emotional and bodily changes, and evolving perspectives. Sometimes, you may notice "aha" moments—sudden realizations that the old story about yourself is no longer running the show. At other times, the shifts might be subtle and gradual.

If, during installation, you become stuck or the positive cognition doesn't increase in believability after several sets, this is normal and provides important feedback. Discuss any doubts, blocks, or resistance with your therapist; sometimes, revisiting earlier phases or strengthening coping skills is helpful before returning to installation.

Practical Tips for Maximizing the Benefits of Phase 5

- Be patient. Sometimes it takes several sessions for a positive cognition to "stick."
- Use your worksheet consistently to anchor physical, emotional, and cognitive shifts.
- Share openly with your therapist if you struggle to find a positive statement that feels right.
- Continue practicing self-care and grounding skills developed in earlier phases, especially if difficult emotions surface unexpectedly.

Phase 5 is a pivotal step toward consolidating the gains made in EMDR. By identifying, refining, and tracking a positive belief, you support your mind in assigning new meaning to old memories. Using the checklist, VOC progress forms, supportive statement guidelines, correlation grid, and worksheets provided, you maximize insight and accelerate the installation process. As you document shifts in belief, emotion, sensation, and imagery, you'll see your progress, build confidence, and lay the groundwork for deeper integration and healing.

Phase 6—Body Scan and Detection of Residual Distress

In EMDR therapy, Phase 6 serves as a critical checkpoint before moving into the closure and reevaluation stages. After the desensitization of distressing memories and the installation of positive beliefs, this phase evaluates whether any residual distress remains in your body.

Integrating body awareness not only accelerates lasting healing but also highlights subtle tension or discomfort that may signal unfinished processing. This chapter will guide you step-by-step through how to use body scan worksheets, checklists, and tables to identify, document, and address physical sensations, empowering you to actively participate in your own healing process.

Body Scan Worksheet for Tracking Physical Sensations

The body scan is a focused exercise where you attend closely to your body, from head to toe, searching for any sensations that stand out as unpleasant, tense, or unresolved. The purpose of this scan is not just to "notice" sensations but to document them systematically and share relevant findings with your therapist. This structured approach makes it much easier for both you and your therapist to pinpoint lingering issues that require attention before concluding the EMDR session.

A typical body scan worksheet invites you to:

1. Close your eyes and bring to mind the originally targeted memory, along with the positive cognition you've been working to install.
2. Move your attention slowly through your body, starting at the top of your head and progressing downward forehead, eyes, jaw, neck, shoulders, arms, chest, stomach, lower back, hips, legs, down to your toes.
3. As you encounter any sensations (tightness, tingling, heaviness, numbness, pain, or warmth), note the location and quality.

Table 12: Example Worksheet

Body Part	Sensation Noted (if any)	Intensity (0-10)	Description/Notes
Jaw	Tension	4	Feels clenched, slight ache
Chest	Warmth	2	Comfortable, slight heartbeat felt
Stomach	Fluttering	6	Nervous, unsettled
Right shoulder	Heaviness	5	Mildly sore, wants to move

This worksheet is filled out during the scan and can be revisited in future sessions to monitor change over time. Remember, the intensity scale is subjective, use it to compare your own sensations from session to session, not to judge or "grade" your progress harshly.

Checklist for common somatic responses and methods to address residual discomfort

Somatic (bodily) responses are signals from the nervous system that may indicate incomplete processing. Not all discomfort represents a problem; some mild sensations are normal and pass quickly. However, significant or stuck somatic reactions should be acknowledged and managed.

Common somatic responses during the body scan include:

- Muscle tightness or tension (in jaw, shoulders, back)
- Tingling or numbness (especially in hands, arms, legs)
- Heaviness or sense of weight in limbs or chest
- Felt temperature changes (hot, cold flashes)
- Stomach "fluttering" or queasiness
- Rapid heartbeat or shallow breathing

Practical methods for addressing residual discomfort:

- Bring the sensation to your therapist's attention so it can be targeted with further bilateral stimulation
- Use grounding or relaxation exercises practised in earlier phases (deep breaths, Safe Place imagery)

- Gently move or stretch if tension is mild and not overwhelming
- If the sensation persists after several attempts at processing, it may indicate an underlying aspect that requires additional EMDR work in subsequent sessions

Use this checklist as a quick-reference alongside your worksheet, so you don't overlook subtle but meaningful signals.

Table for documenting new areas of tension or relief post-processing

The body scan also captures positive shifts: areas of relief, warmth, or relaxation, which can be just as telling as discomfort. Documenting both emerges as essential for tracking your progress and providing your therapist with useful feedback.

After completion of bilateral stimulation and installation:

Table 13: Documenting Template

Body Part	Pre-Processing Sensation	Post-Processing Change	Relief or New Tension?	Notes
Shoulders	Heavy, tense (7/10)	Looser, relaxed (2/10)	Relief	Tension mostly gone
Lower back	No sensation	Mild ache (3/10)	New tension	Noticed after memory revisited
Chest	Tight, anxious	Warmth,	Relief	Felt easy to

	(5/10)	open (1/10)		breathe
Left leg	Tingly (3/10)	Tingly (3/10)	No change	Watch for persistence

By populating this table each session, you and your therapist can discern patterns—identifying which bodily tensions fade with successful processing and which may need additional focus. If new areas of discomfort emerge post-processing, they should be reported and, if necessary, assigned as future targets for EMDR work.

Boundary guidelines for reporting strong or stuck sensations to the therapist

It's natural for residual sensations to surface during a thorough body scan, but it is crucial to recognize your role and your limits in resolving these on your own. The following guidelines help create safety and transparency:

- If a physical sensation registers at moderate to high intensity (typically 5 out of 10 or higher), or if it feels "immovable" or increases when you focus attention on it, report this directly to your therapist.
- Strong sensations accompanied by emotion (e.g., nausea with sadness, pounding heart with fear) should be discussed before the session continues to closure.
- If a sensation is confusing, triggers memories, or makes it hard to stay present, clarify these feelings with your therapist rather than ignoring or "pushing through."

- It's always appropriate to ask for a pause, grounding technique, or brief bilateral stimulation set to process the area further if distress does not substantially decrease.
- Avoid self-judgment about what is "valid" to report. Every sensation is informative and may guide the next phase of healing.

Ultimately, your therapist is trained to help you interpret these signals and decide whether additional processing is needed immediately or in future sessions.

Body scan completion checklist for verifying resolution of identified discomforts

Before closing the session or moving to closure protocols, use a completion checklist to verify that significant areas of distress have been addressed. This systematic approach ensures nothing important is overlooked.

Use this checklist for your body scan wrap-up:

- Have I scanned my entire body, deliberately and without rushing, from head to toe?
- Did I notice any area where a sensation stood out as uncomfortable, painful, tense, or "odd"?
- Did I document each of these sensations, their intensity, and quality on my worksheet or table?

- Have I discussed all lingering or persistent sensations with my therapist, even if I felt unsure or embarrassed?
- Did my therapist and I use further bilateral stimulation or other supportive techniques to "clear" these sensations as much as possible?
- Do I feel a general sense of relief, relaxation, or neutrality regarding the target memory and my body?
- Is it clear which (if any) areas need further attention in upcoming sessions?
- Have I completed post-scan documentation of all new areas of relief or remaining tension for session tracking?
- Do I understand my next steps if a sensation reappears between sessions (e.g., when to use grounding skills, when to reach out for support)?

This checklist provides confidence that you have honored both the mind and body's responses and that lingering distress will not go unaddressed. It also prepares you to participate in later phases, such as closure and reevaluation, by establishing a baseline for body awareness and symptom tracking.

Integrating the Body Scan into Your EMDR Journey

The body scan phase is a practical, empowering step in your EMDR treatment. It bridges cognitive and physiological progress, ensuring both are brought into conscious awareness before closure. By systematically using the body scan worksheet, somatic response checklist, documentation table, boundary guidelines, and completion checklist, you become an active collaborator in your own therapeutic process.

<u>As you incorporate these tools, remember:</u>

- Residual body sensations provide important information about unfinished processing or emerging targets.
- Tracking and reporting real-time shifts gives you and your therapist the data needed to personalize your EMDR sessions and maximize healing outcomes.
- Safety and transparency are always prioritized—report what you notice, and use all available support if strong feelings or sensations arise.

Completion of the body scan in Phase 6 sets the stage for the final steps of EMDR closure and reevaluation by confirming that the mind and body are as clear and settled as possible regarding the targeted memory. Using the simple but structured worksheets and checklists described above, you ensure that progress is captured, discomfort is addressed, and each EMDR session builds securely on the last.

Phase 7—Closure and Self-Care Strategies

Phase 7 marks the structured conclusion of each session, serving dual roles: ensuring emotional stability before you leave and equipping you with self-care tools to manage any ongoing or delayed reactions to memory processing. Just as the earlier phases prepared and guided you through intense emotional work, this phase is carefully constructed to help you leave sessions feeling grounded, safe, and empowered to continue healing between appointments.

A thorough closure routine and personalized self-care plan are especially important because EMDR can bring up new thoughts or feelings for a period after the session ends.

End-of-session grounding exercise checklist

Following the body scan, your therapist will guide you through one or more closure routines to firmly transition you from processing back to the here-and-now. These exercises serve to stabilize mood, lower arousal levels, and enhance your sense of present safety. Many closure routines are direct extensions of coping skills, relaxation techniques, or resource exercises learned earlier in therapy. Having a step-by-step checklist helps you actively participate and recall the sequence should you need it outside sessions.

Here is a sample end-of-session grounding checklist:

1. Name five objects you can see, four sounds you can hear, and three physical sensations you notice (such as the feel of your chair, your feet on the floor, or your breath moving in and out).
2. Practice slow, deep breathing: inhale for a count of four, hold for two, exhale for six. Repeat 3–5 cycles.
3. Use your established Safe Place imagery, close your eyes and vividly recall your Safe Place, imagining sights, sounds, textures, scents, and feelings of comfort experienced there.
4. Notice and rate your current level of distress (using the SUD—Subjective Units of Distress—scale) and compare this to the beginning and peak of your session.
5. Remind yourself of your chosen coping statement or positive cognition, such as "I am safe now," or "I can handle my feelings."
6. Stretch or gently move your body to reestablish physical awareness.
7. Confirm with your therapist that you feel present, steady, and ready to transition out of the session.

When you follow each step, you intentionally signal to your mind and body that active memory processing has ended for the day, that you are rooted in the present, and that you have resources to manage any emotional after-effects.

Template for daily self-care plans incorporating coping tools practiced in therapy

EMDR can lead to subtle or pronounced shifts in emotions and bodily sensations between sessions. To support continued healing and minimize distress, it is recommended that you follow a personalized daily self-care plan especially in the days immediately following active EMDR processing. The most effective plans integrate skills and exercises introduced during earlier phases, helping you reinforce your resilience and sense of control.

Fill out your daily plan using the following template:

Morning:

- Grounding exercise (choose: body scan, mindful breathing, or Safe Place imagery)
- Intention for the day (such as "Stay gentle with myself")
- Identify one realistic, nurturing activity (e.g., making a healthy breakfast, taking a walk)

Afternoon:

- Check in on mood and body sensations; rate any distress on a 0–10 scale
- Use a resource technique if needed (e.g., butterfly hug, brief bilateral stimulation with tapping hands or feet)
- Take a short break to stretch, hydrate, or rest

Evening:

- Reflect on wins (even small ones) and challenges faced during the day
- Use a closure exercise: slow breathing, muscle relaxation, or gentle self-talk
- Prepare for restful sleep (limit screen time, create a calm environment)
- If strong feelings remain: jot them in your closure worksheet

This template can be tailored to your schedule, preferences, and unique stress patterns. By weaving specific EMDR skills such as grounding, Safe Place, and resource development into daily routines, you anchor the therapeutic gains and reduce the risk of emotional overwhelm between sessions.

List of signals indicating when to use additional grounding or resource techniques at home

While many people finish EMDR sessions feeling stable, it is entirely normal for distress or unsettling thoughts to surface in the hours or days afterward. To manage these moments proactively, it is essential to understand which signals suggest you should pause and use grounding or resource techniques outside of therapy.

Key signals include:

- ***Sudden or persistent emotional distress***, such as anxiety, sadness, irritability, or anger, that feels linked to issues processed in your recent EMDR session
- ***Noticeable changes in body sensations***—tightness, tingling, heaviness, or restlessness that do not fade with rest or distraction
- ***Difficulty staying present or "zoning out"*** (dissociation), especially if you feel confused about what's happening in your mind or body
- ***Flooding of distressing memories***, images, or intrusive thoughts related to earlier EMDR processing
- ***Trouble falling or staying asleep*** because your mind is preoccupied with session material
- ***Urges to isolate***, avoid daily tasks, or engage in unhelpful, impulsive behaviors to manage discomfort

When any of these signals emerge, pause and intentionally use one or more coping skills practiced in therapy:

- Grounding your senses (5-4-3-2-1 technique)
- Safe Place visualization
- Deep, slow, rhythmic breathing
- Physical activity walking, stretching, gentle movement
- Repeating a personal coping statement

If distress persists after several rounds of self-help, or if you feel unable to manage powerful emotions, it is appropriate to reach out to your therapist for support before the next session.

Closure worksheet to log remaining thoughts, feelings, or concerns post-session

A core part of EMDR closure involves documenting your internal experience after the session. This process provides valuable insights for your therapist and keeps you actively engaged in noticing how you are feeling, what is resolved, and what might remain unfinished. Use the closure worksheet as soon as possible after your session, and revisit it if new reactions arise that you wish to track.

Sample closure worksheet:

1. What thoughts or images linger most strongly from today's session?
2. Are there any unresolved feelings, body sensations, or questions that emerged during or after the session?

3. Rate your current distress/tension level (0–10) and note the location or quality of any physical discomfort.
4. Did you use a coping tool after the session? Which one, and was it effective?
5. Are there any memories, concerns, or reactions you need to discuss with your therapist at the start of your next session?
6. Have any new insights or positive shifts occurred since the session ended?
7. Additional notes to self (reminders, encouragement, or intentions for self-care).

Recording answers creates an ongoing dialogue between client and therapist. This approach supports tracking progress, anticipating challenges, and personalizing future sessions.

Framework for creating a personalized coping plan for managing after-effects

Closure in EMDR is not only about ending a session on a calm note, but also about preventing unmanageable escalation or distress between appointments. Developing a coping plan in collaboration with your therapist gives you a clear roadmap for responding to post-processing effects. This plan outlines both your personal warning signals and the strategies most likely to help in those situations.

Use the following framework to guide your plan:

1. ***List your most common distress signals*** (e.g., headache, racing thoughts, intrusive memories, restlessness).
2. ***Identify early warning signs*** subtle shifts that tell you distress might escalate.
3. ***Choose 2–3 grounding or resource techniques*** that reliably bring comfort or stability.
4. ***Develop a stepwise response***:
    - Step 1: Recognize and name the feeling or sensation.
    - Step 2: Rate the intensity (0–10) and decide whether to pause and use a skill.
    - Step 3: Practice a grounding skill for 3–5 minutes. Note the impact.
    - Step 4: If relief is partial or fleeting, switch to another resource technique or try a brief physical reset (walk, stretch, drink water).
5. ***Make a safety contact plan*** to decide who to reach out to (therapist, support person) if strong distress does not resolve with self-help strategies.
6. ***Write out reminders***: "It is normal to have emotional waves after EMDR. I have effective tools and support. I don't have to go through this alone."

Continue using the closure worksheet after each session to update your coping plan, noting which tools are most effective and what new challenges arise for you personally.

Phase 7 is a pivotal transition in EMDR treatment, ensuring you leave each session feeling attended to, empowered, and ready to safeguard your well-being outside the therapist's office. End-of-session grounding, personalized daily care, clear signals for self-intervention, systematic logging of your experience, and the development of a tailored coping plan all work together to maximize healing while minimizing risks of discomfort or emotional volatility post-session.

Consistently applying the practical checklists, worksheets, and frameworks outlined here, you become an expert in your own process able to anticipate, notice, and respond to whatever EMDR brings up between sessions. As a result, you provide stability for yourself while giving your therapist the detailed, nuanced information needed to fine-tune your therapy, phase by phase. This partnership between structured closure routines and personalized self-care forms the heart of safe, effective EMDR therapy and prepares you for future growth and resolution.

Phase 8—Reevaluation and Session Outcome Tracking

The completion of the closure phase in EMDR therapy signals not the end, but a crucial turning point: Phase 8, known as Reevaluation. This final phase is where you and your therapist methodically track and reflect on changes that began earlier in the process, assess lasting shifts, and identify areas needing renewed focus.

With careful documentation using progress logs, structured worksheets, and summary sheets Phase 8 helps you keep steady momentum toward your goals, ensuring that therapeutic gains are recognized, integrated, and, where necessary, extended through targeted follow-up.

Progress log for noting ongoing changes and new targets for future sessions

Continuing your EMDR journey, a dedicated progress log is essential. This living document allows you to record both subtle and dramatic shifts, stemming not only from the immediate aftereffects of recent sessions but also from cumulative changes in your emotions, thoughts, behaviors, and relationships. **Use your progress log to capture:**

- Emerging feelings of relief, hope, or mastery that develop days or weeks after active EMDR processing
- Fluctuations in distress related to past target memories
- Recognition of new or previously unnoticed memories or beliefs that may surface as your original targets are resolved
- Goals or issues you wish to address in future sessions, even if they feel only loosely connected to your original concerns

Frequent, open logging ensures that your therapy remains responsive to your evolving needs. Some patients find it helpful to set aside a few minutes each evening or after significant emotional events to add to the log. Regular entries not only reinforce your engagement but provide your therapist with high-value information for tailoring your treatment plan. This approach creates a shared roadmap, giving structure and clarity to future sessions and increasing your sense of agency in the healing process.

Weekly or session-based worksheet for reevaluating SUD and VOC scores

A hallmark of EMDR therapy is the use of simple, effective rating scales to track your progress through each memory or cognition targeted in treatment. Two primary rating tools are particularly important to revisit during reevaluation:

- ***SUD (Subjective Units of Distress) scale***: rates your current level of distress on a scale from 0 (no distress) to 10 (highest possible distress) when recalling target memories.
- ***VOC (Validity of Cognition) scale***: measures how true a chosen positive belief feels to you on a scale from 1 (completely false) to 7 (completely true).

After your initial processing of a target memory, use a weekly or per-session worksheet to re-rate both SUD and VOC for that specific memory. Your therapist will likely revisit these ratings at the start of each new session, but you can also track them independently between appointments. **Noting these scores:**

- Provides concrete evidence of reduced distress and strengthened positive beliefs
- Highlights any residual emotional charge or areas where positive cognitions do not yet feel fully integrated
- Supports informed decisions about whether a memory is truly "resolved" or if additional processing is needed

Reevaluation worksheet should include the date, the memory or belief being rated, SUD and VOC scores, and brief notes on any changes in emotion, physical sensations, or thoughts tied to that target. You will create a visible map of your healing trajectory, reinforcing progress and identifying lingering patterns that warrant follow-up.

Template for recording insights, dreams, or shifts in real-world behavior between sessions

Memory processing in EMDR often continues subconsciously in the days and weeks between appointments. It is common for people to notice:

- New insights about their past or present after periods of reflection or sudden emotional clarity
- Dreams or unexpected imagery relating to session material, which may signal ongoing integration or release of previously "stuck" material
- Observable shifts in behaviors, such as feeling less avoidant in certain situations, improved self-care, or more effective assertiveness in relationships

Maintain a dedicated template for jotting down these experiences as they arise. Template might include sections like:

1. Date and time of the observation
2. Brief description of dream, insight, or change in behavior

3. Connection (if any) to session targets, emotions, or positive cognitions
4. Intensity of the change or how significant it feels, rated on a simple 1–5 scale
5. Questions or reflections to discuss with your therapist during the next session

Written notes help ensure valuable changes or developments are not lost in the shuffle of daily life, and they allow for a richer, more nuanced discussion in therapy. Your therapist may use these notes to adjust future targets, explore newly emerging themes, or celebrate important wins.

Checklist for identifying when memories or symptoms re-emerge and require further processing

Despite significant progress, it is not unusual for certain memories or symptoms to resurface, especially as deeper layers of past trauma unravel. Building a checklist helps you monitor for such instances and discern whether they require renewed therapeutic attention. **Signals that an issue may need to be revisited include:**

- Sudden spikes in SUD scores when recalling a "resolved" memory
- Return of distressing dreams, intrusive images, or bodily reactions associated with previously processed material

- Onset of new or intensified avoidance behaviors around themes addressed in earlier sessions
- Difficulties in integrating new positive beliefs, e.g., you intellectually "know" something is true, but emotionally it does not feel that way

To use the checklist effectively:

1. Rate your SUD and VOC for each previously addressed memory or belief at least once per week for the first month after it was processed.
2. Note any increases in distress, self-doubt, or negative self-talk related to session themes.
3. Log any surprising physical symptoms (such as headaches, stomachaches, or muscle tension) that arise in contexts connected to EMDR targets.
4. Identify any new situational triggers that seem to re-activate old patterns of distress.
5. Discuss flagged items with your therapist to determine whether further bilateral stimulation, cognitive restructuring, or other interventions might be helpful.

Tackling resurfacing material promptly can prevent regression and ensures a flexible, individualized path to healing.

Summary sheet for periodic review of overall therapy progress and unresolved issues

At regular intervals, often every four to six sessions, or at key transitional points in your EMDR treatment summarizing your progress is invaluable. This summary sheet brings together data and impressions from your progress log, rating worksheets, insight templates, and reemergence checklists. **Its primary functions are:**

- To review resolved targets, measuring sustained decreases in SUD and increases in VOC scores for each
- To highlight targets or themes that still evoke distress or remain insufficiently addressed
- To identify patterns in what helps you shift toward healing, and what interferes with progress
- To prioritize unresolved memories, beliefs, or behaviors for upcoming sessions
- To support collaborative decision-making with your therapist about ending, maintaining, or adjusting your EMDR plan

Sections in your summary sheet should include:

- A table of target memories processed, dates, original and current SUD/VOC scores

- Notable successes (significant score reductions, positive life changes, improved coping)
- Areas needing review or further work (memories with lingering distress, recurring symptoms)
- Open notes on feelings about therapy, remaining concerns, or personal growth reflections

Committing to a structured review not only sharpens your awareness of what's working and what's not but ensures that EMDR treatment proceeds with ongoing intention and personalization.

Integrating Reevaluation Tools into Your EMDR Experience

The strength of EMDR therapy lies not only in what you accomplish during active memory processing, but in how well you and your therapist track, confirm, and build upon those gains over time. Structured self-evaluation progress logs, rating scales, insight templates, remediation checklists, and summary reviews collects concrete evidence of change, uncovers continuing challenges, and guides subsequent therapy with clarity and purpose.

<u>**This ongoing documentation empowers you to:**</u>

- Notice incremental progress sometimes imperceptible in the moment when looking back over weeks or months

- Identify setbacks early, before they undermine your morale or the effectiveness of therapy
- Sharpen your self-awareness, resilience, and commitment to healing

If you ever feel unsure about rating your experiences, logging insights, or using the worksheets suggested here, remember: your entries are not "tests" to pass, but essential tools for reflection. There is no right or wrong way to experience change. What matters is consistency and honesty in tracking your journey.

Phase 8 transforms the EMDR process from a series of sessions into a continuous, adaptive system for healing. The more thoroughly you approach outcome tracking, the more equipped you become to claim (and sustain) meaningful change. EMDR's evidence-based structure, guided by ongoing feedback and robust self-documentation, enables not just symptom reduction but genuine, lasting transformation.

Managing Challenges and Maximizing EMDR Benefits

Successfully navigating EMDR therapy is often as much about effectively managing challenges as it is about participating in the structured 8-phase process. As you move through the phases, you may encounter moments of discomfort, difficulties in emotional regulation, or even obstacles that interfere with progress. Recognizing these difficulties early and applying targeted troubleshooting strategies will help you maintain momentum and maximize the healing potential of EMDR.

Catalog of common difficulty signals and troubleshooting strategies

Because EMDR works by directly engaging memories and emotions, temporary increases in distress or unexpected reactions are normal. Identifying and understanding these signals is the first step toward overcoming them. **Some of the most common signs of difficulty during EMDR include:**

- Emotional flooding, where overwhelming feelings arise during or after sessions
- Sudden spikes in anxiety, irritability, or agitation between appointments
- Unproductive looping or feeling "stuck" on a particular memory or negative thought despite repeated processing
- Physical symptoms such as headaches, fatigue, or muscle tension following sessions
- Intrusive memories, nightmares, or new avoidant behaviors emerging during treatment

If you notice these signals, consider the following troubleshooting strategies:

1. ***Pause and ground yourself***: During overwhelming moments in a session, ask for a break. Use grounding tools from the preparation phase (such as slow breathing or Safe Place imagery).
2. ***Track patterns***: Keep a written log of when and how symptoms arise. Patterns may point to specific triggers or therapy-interfering behaviors.
3. ***Communicate openly***: Bring up all difficulty signals with your therapist. Even subtle changes might carry important information for adjusting your therapeutic plan.
4. ***Practice skill-building***: Revisit coping exercises from earlier EMDR phases if distress is high.

5. ***Adjust session pace***: If you're repeatedly overwhelmed, it may be necessary to slow the pace of memory processing or revisit earlier stabilization skills before proceeding.

Many EMDR patients naturally face isolated periods of difficulty, especially when old coping mechanisms are challenged. These moments are not signs of failure, but invitations to use your growing skills and resources, supported by collaborative therapist guidance.

Ruleset for managing overwhelming emotions during and between sessions

Managing strong emotional reactions is central to making safe, effective progress in EMDR therapy. During both sessions and the days between, stick to a clear ruleset for emotional self-care:

- ***Recognize escalation***: Notice early physiological signs of distress, such as racing pulse, sweating, or rapid, negative thought spirals.
- ***Signal to your therapist***: If in session, immediately alert your therapist when overwhelm builds.
- ***Activate grounding***: Shift attention to the present by focusing on physical sensations, breathing exercises, or visualizing your safe place, a core tool introduced in early EMDR phases.

- ***Use bilateral activities***: Calm the nervous system by mimicking bilateral stimulation at home alternating tapping on knees or squeezing a small object in each hand, while recalling positive images.
- ***Schedule self-checks***: Set reminders during the week to check in on mood and physical state; note any persistent distress in your therapy worksheets.
- ***Limit triggers***: Reduce exposure to particularly distressing situations or media during intensive EMDR processing windows.
- ***Revisit stabilization skills***: Engage in relaxation, mindfulness, or distraction techniques practiced in Phase 2 whenever distress rises.
- ***Delay processing new material***: Do not attempt to self-process additional traumatic memories at home; new targets should only be addressed in collaboration with your therapist.

For persistent or severe emotional overwhelm that does not subside with coping strategies, contact your therapist or use crisis resources listed later in this chapter.

List of therapist communication questions and self-advocacy tools

Honest, ongoing communication with your therapist is vital for a successful EMDR experience. Many difficulties arise not from what is processed, but from what goes unspoken.

Maximize your role as an active participant using the following questions and self-advocacy tools:

Therapist Communication Questions:

- Can we revisit coping skills if I begin to feel overwhelmed in or between sessions?
- How can I recognize and report when I am "stuck" or looping on a memory?
- What should I do if intrusive memories or dreams occur outside sessions?
- Should we adjust session pace or target selection if current material feels too intense?
- Can you help me understand why I might have new symptoms since beginning EMDR?
- What options exist for extra support if difficulties persist outside therapy hours?
- May I request to pause or slow down processing anytime if it becomes too distressing?

Self-Advocacy Tools:

- Use your worksheets to bring concrete examples of symptoms, reactions, or questions to each session.
- Assert the right to take breaks or shift focus if emotional intensity spikes.
- Ask for periodic review of goals, progress, and readiness to target new material.

- Request additional Phase 2 stabilization practice before moving forward if needed.
- Set clear boundaries regarding topics or memories you are not ready to address.

These strategies not only safeguard your emotional well-being, they support a stronger therapeutic alliance and a more tailored treatment path.

Worksheet for identifying and tracking therapy-interfering behaviors

Interruptions to EMDR progress can stem from both recallable events and subtle, ongoing behaviors. Using a worksheet to track "therapy-interfering behaviors" brings clarity and structure to managing obstacles. This worksheet typically covers:

- ***Avoidance***: Canceling or delaying sessions, withholding information, or unconsciously steering conversation away from challenging material.
- ***Intellectualization***: Focusing excessively on analysis, facts, or logic to avoid emotion.
- ***Self-criticism***: Persistent negative self-talk interfering with engagement.
- ***Numbing behaviors***: Substance use, compulsive distractions (e.g., excessive screen time), or other activities used to block emotions.

- ***Disconnection***: Difficulty feeling present, engaging in daydreaming, or blanking out when challenging material arises.

Table 14: Therapy-Interfering Behaviors Tracking Worksheet

Date	Ex: 03/03		
Behavior Observed	Arriving 15m late		
Context or Trigger	Traffic/Anxiety		
Intensity (1-5)	3		
Impact on Session	Shortened time		
Steps Taken	Discussed barrier		
Response/ Result	Set earlier alarm		

By logging these behaviors over time, you become aware of patterns and can partner with your therapist to develop customized coping strategies and session plans. Regularly reviewing this worksheet together helps identify if new skills, different pacing, or renewed focus on stabilization is required.

Emergency contacts and resource list for crisis support outside sessions

While the majority of EMDR work occurs in carefully facilitated sessions, emotional distress can sometimes escalate unexpectedly outside scheduled appointments. It is essential to have an emergency plan and resource list prepared before starting intensive trauma processing.

Key Elements of Your Crisis Resource Plan:

- ***Primary Therapist Contact***: Write down your therapist's direct phone number and regular office hours.
- ***Emergency Backup Line***: If your therapist is unavailable, know whom to call within the practice or clinic.
- ***National Crisis Helplines***: Save trusted resources such as the National Suicide Prevention Lifeline, crisis text lines, or other mental health helplines that offer 24/7 support.
- ***Local Emergency Services***: Have your local mental health urgent care and hospital emergency department locations, addresses, and phone numbers accessible.
- ***Trusted Support Network***: Identify friends, family members, or peer supporters who understand your EMDR process and can provide non-judgmental, calming presence during difficult moments.
- ***Personal Safety Plan***: Outline step-by-step instructions for removing yourself from unsafe situations, engaging in grounding exercises, and reaching out for help.

Table 15: Crisis Resource List Template

Resource	Contact Information	Availability	Purpose
National Suicide Prevention Lifeline	988 or https://988lifeline.org	24/7	Free, confidential support for people in distress
Crisis Text Line	Text HOME to 741741	24/7	Text-based support for any crisis
Local Emergency Services	911	24/7	For immediate danger or medical emergencies
Nearest Hospital Emergency Room	[Insert local hospital info]	24/7	Go directly in case of urgent need
Trusted Friend/ Family Member	[Insert name & phone number]	Varies	Identified personal crisis contact
Primary Care Provider	[Insert provider name & contact]	Office hours	Medical or mental health support

Make multiple copies of your resource list: one for your wallet, one in your phone, and one posted somewhere visible at home. Share this plan with a trusted contact so that you are never navigating a crisis alone.

EMDR is structured to help you move deliberately through each phase, building skills and resilience for life beyond therapy. But the journey is rarely perfectly linear; difficulty signals will occasionally arise, emotions can become overwhelming, and behavioral obstacles may surface. By proactively cataloging signals, using structured troubleshooting, advocating with your therapist, and relying on personalized worksheets, you stay engaged and safe throughout the process.

Maximizing the benefits of EMDR is a collaborative, adaptive process. Each worksheet and checklist you complete, each signal you bring to your therapist's attention, and each step you take toward emotionally safe engagement increases your capacity for deep and lasting healing. Remember, every moment of difficulty is an opportunity to practice resourcefulness, refine self-care, and strengthen your partnership with your therapist.

Should you ever find yourself struggling to implement these strategies or unsure how best to use the tools outlined here, discuss your concerns openly during your session. Your EMDR therapy is uniquely yours. Let these resources empower you to navigate challenges with confidence, knowing support and structure are ready whenever needed.

Conclusion

As your EMDR journey moves beyond the structure of active therapy sessions, the tools and strategies you have practiced, especially tracking, checklists, and worksheets become essential companions on your healing path. These resources were designed not only to help you organize memories, skills, and session outcomes, but also to empower you with the confidence and clarity to take ownership of your progress both within and beyond the therapy office.

Tracking forms and checklists serve as a personalized roadmap, providing step-by-step structure to your EMDR work. By recording SUD (Subjective Units of Distress) and VOC (Validity of Cognition) scores, noting shifts in emotional or physical responses, and logging self-care strategies, you have built a clear picture of your healing over time. Worksheets for each phase of EMDR make progress visible and tangible, supporting a sense of accomplishment through concrete evidence of change.

This ongoing self-documentation streamlines complicated healing work, transforming an overwhelming process into a series of manageable steps and decisions. With each completed tracker or checklist, you reinforce your commitment and empower yourself to maintain momentum even in the face of setbacks or uncertainty.

Sustaining your gains after therapy concludes is a key part of the EMDR process. Continued self-evaluation ensures that the coping skills and insights you have developed remain accessible and useful as new challenges arise. Periodically revisiting your readiness checklists, session worksheets, or self-care plans helps you identify areas where additional support or a skills refresher might be needed.

Many individuals find that regularly completing body scan worksheets or monitoring emotional distress on a simplified SUD scale keeps them attuned to early warning signs of stress, giving them the opportunity to use stabilization techniques before old patterns resurface.

To extend the benefits of EMDR into everyday life, integrate learned self-care and grounding strategies into your regular routines. Short daily check-ins using worksheet templates adapted from the therapy process can help track mood, intrusive thoughts, or physical sensations. Simple practices, such as guided safe place imagery, bilateral self-stimulation (tapping or auditory exercises), and rehearsed positive self-talk, support emotional regulation long after formal sessions end. Should you notice a return of distressing symptoms or unresolved memories, refer to your EMDR progress logs to determine if these issues have been processed before or warrant new attention.

Ongoing self-monitoring is greatly enhanced by scheduled follow-up reviews and maintenance sessions, which can be arranged with your therapist as needed. Some individuals find it helpful to plan periodic "booster" sessions perhaps quarterly or semi-annually to check in on progress, revisit coping tools, and process any new or resurfacing memories. Discuss with your therapist whether maintenance appointments, brief check-ins, or even email updates might provide the level of support you require to maintain your gains while living more independently.

In addition to professional follow-ups, independent self-care practices can keep you grounded and resilient. Continue using the coping worksheets, progress-tracking charts, and readiness checklists provided in this guide as part of your regular self-reflection routine. Keep these resources easily accessible whether as printed pages in a binder or digital documents on your phone so that you can capture emotional changes, insights, or concerns as they arise. Remember that your EMDR journey is ongoing and uniquely yours; the skills, documentation habits, and self-awareness you have developed are lasting tools for lifelong healing and growth.

FAQs

How do I know if I'm ready to begin EMDR therapy?

Deciding when to start Eye Movement Desensitization and Reprocessing (EMDR) therapy is a crucial first step. Readiness involves more than just willingness; it includes having emotional stability and support. Generally, you're considered ready if you can manage strong feelings without becoming overwhelmed, have basic calming strategies, and trust your ability to seek help if needed.

Feeling pain or discomfort about your past is normal; however, if you feel persistently overwhelmed, it may be best to focus on stabilization first. During the initial phase, your therapist will assess your readiness, review your coping tools and support systems, and help clarify your goals. This collaborative process ensures your safety and success.

What if I feel emotionally overwhelmed during or between sessions?

It's common to feel overwhelmed during or after EMDR sessions, especially when processing difficult memories. EMDR includes a preparation phase where you and your therapist practice calming techniques, such as visualization or grounding. If you become overwhelmed in a session, let your therapist know they can pause the process and support you in using coping strategies.

If distress arises between sessions, use the tools you've practiced, like deep breathing or safe place imagery. Keeping a log of your emotional responses to share with your therapist can be helpful. If intense distress persists, contact your therapist to discuss extra support or additional stabilization before continuing.

Are all memories or issues suitable for EMDR processing?

Not all memories or experiences are immediately suitable for EMDR. You and your therapist will review your history to select target memories that cause current symptoms but aren't so overwhelming as to destabilize you. Recent trauma, severe untreated mental illness, or difficulty maintaining safety may require further preparation or different interventions before EMDR begins.

While EMDR is validated for processing traumatic memories, it may not be the best approach for memories causing no current distress or for ongoing situations. Your therapist will help tailor your treatment plan to ensure safe and effective processing.

Is eye movement required, or can other forms of bilateral stimulation be used?

Bilateral stimulation is essential in EMDR, but it does not have to involve only eye movements. Alternatives like tapping, hand-held buzzers, or listening to alternating sounds are also effective. Your therapist will discuss these options and help you find what feels most comfortable. The goal is rhythmic, alternating stimulation of both sides of the body or brain, which supports memory processing. The method can be adapted to your preferences and any physical needs while following the EMDR protocol.

How can I track progress if I have trouble remembering session details?

It's normal for session details to fade, especially after intense work. Tracking progress can be done through session logs or worksheets, where you note distress levels, emotional shifts, and insights soon after sessions. Even brief notes about emotions, images, or sensations can reveal change over time. Discussing progress with your therapist at the start of each session is also helpful. If tracking remains difficult, consider tools like voice memos or mood charts to make it easier.

Does EMDR work for anxiety and other issues besides trauma?

While EMDR is best known for treating post-traumatic stress disorder (PTSD), research suggests it can also help with anxiety, depression, phobias, and some aspects of grief or chronic pain especially when symptoms relate to unresolved past experiences. Your therapist will determine if EMDR fits your needs and may combine it with other approaches, especially for complex or longstanding issues. Open communication about your goals and concerns will help create the best treatment plan for you.

What if I don't feel comfortable with my therapist during EMDR?

A strong, trusting relationship with your therapist is vital for EMDR to be effective. If you feel uncomfortable, discuss your concerns openly whether about pacing, misunderstandings, or specific techniques. Most therapists welcome feedback and will work with you to resolve issues. If discomfort remains, you have the right to seek another provider. Your comfort and safety are the foundation for successful therapy.

References and Helpful Links

SEIDLER, G., WAGNER, F.. (2006). Comparing the efficacy of EMDR and trauma-focused cognitive-behavioral therapy in the treatment of PTSD: a meta-analytic study. Psychological Medicine. https://doi.org/10.1017/s0033291706007963

de Jongh, A., Amann, B., Hofmann, A. et al.. (2019). The Status of EMDR Therapy in the Treatment of Posttraumatic Stress Disorder 30 Years After Its Introduction. Journal of EMDR Practice and Research. https://doi.org/10.1891/1933-3196.13.4.261

Valiente-Gómez, A., Moreno-Alcázar, A., Treen, D. et al.. (2017). EMDR beyond PTSD: A Systematic Literature Review. https://doi.org/10.3389/fpsyg.2017.01668

Lee, C., Cuijpers, P.. (2013). A meta-analysis of the contribution of eye movements in processing emotional memories. https://doi.org/10.1016/j.jbtep.2012.11.001

Carletto, S., Oliva, F., Barnato, M. et al.. (2018). EMDR as Add-On Treatment for Psychiatric and Traumatic Symptoms in Patients with Substance Use Disorder. Frontiers in Psychology. https://doi.org/10.3389/fpsyg.2017.02333

Hase, M.. (2021). The Structure of EMDR Therapy: A Guide for the Therapist. Frontiers in Psychology. https://doi.org/10.3389/fpsyg.2021.660753

Oren, E., Solomon, R.. (2012). EMDR therapy: An overview of its development and mechanisms of action. European Review of Applied Psychology. https://doi.org/10.1016/j.erap.2012.08.005

www.ingramcontent.com/pod-product-compliance
Lightning Source LLC
LaVergne TN
LVHW022009200926
848481LV00007B/2297